ESSENC

MW01603044

BY

R.H. SIN
&
SAMANTHA KING

UNDERWATER MOUNTAINS PUBLISHING
LOS ANGELES, CALIFORNIA

ESSENCE OF OUR ASHES BY SAMANTHA KING AND R.H. SIN

ALL RIGHTS RESERVED.
NO PART OF THIS PUBLICATION MAY BE REPRODUCED,
DISTRIBUTED, OR TRANSMITTED IN ANY FORM OR BY
ANY MEANS, INCLUDING PHOTOCOPYING, RECORDING, OR
OTHER ELECTRONIC OR MECHANICAL METHODS, WITHOUT THE
PRIOR WRITTEN PERMISSION OF THE PUBLISHER, EXCEPT IN
BRIEF QUOTATIONS EMBODIED IN CRITICAL REVIEWS, CITATIONS,
AND LITERARY JOURNALS FOR NONCOMMERCIAL USES
PERMITTED BY COPYRIGHT LAW.

FOR PERMISSION REQUESTS, EMAIL US AT
LEGAL@UNDERWATERMOUNTAINS.BIZ
WITH THE BODY: "ATTENTION: PERMISSIONS COORDINATOR."

THIS IS A WORK OF FICTION.
NO CHARACTER IN THIS WORK IS A REAL PERSON OR BASED ON
A REAL PERSON,
UNLESS NOTED.

COPYRIGHT 2015 © UNDERWATER MOUNTAINS PUBLISHING
WWW.UNDERWATERMOUNTAINS.COM

ESSENCE OF OUR ASHES

R.H. SIN

(12:22am)

while you lay in bed,
questioning the things he does
and says,
stressing over and or debating
whether or not to leave,
waiting by the phone for a text
you won't get,
tired of being tired of his shit,
there's someone planning out a life
that includes a woman like you.

(a significant loss)

weeks after we knew,
you began showing and glowing.
me, I was happy,
telling everyone the good news.
years later, we're still dealing with the loss
of life you were carrying for us.
who knew? our blessing would come
and go so quickly. So soon.

(a woman's strength)

she's struggled,
she's been hurt,
and there were times where
she's felt weak,
yet she remains strong.
she's winning battles
that no one knows about
simply because
she chooses to smile
through it all.
she is you.

(an hourglass, too late)

you care. you care more than anyone else has.
yet they'll never realize it until they've lost
what could've been the best thing to happen to them.
we're always waiting until it's too late,
taking time for granted until time runs out.

(beautiful destruction)

there's beauty in destruction and chaos—
the way she smiles while battling her demons,
the way her heart becomes stronger soon after
being broken.
they try to steal her sanity, but she finds peace
within the storm.
look how ugly it can get, and look
how beautiful she remains.

(defining a queen)

she made pain look beautiful.
she found peace among the chaos.
she wore a smile
in situations where most would cry.
she held the weight of the world
on her shoulders and never complained.
she is strong, she is queen,
she is you.

"Illa"

she was love,
she was attitude,
she was strength,
wrapped in beauty.
she was the type
of woman who struck
fear in the heart's
of weak men.
she was the type of woman
that only a strong man
could adore.
she's always been you.

(illusions in love)

for me ,
love has always been an illusion.
i'd stumble upon what appeared
to be genuine
only to discover
those claims of truly feeling something real
were simply false.
my heart no longer trusts the texture
of those three words anymore
or at least not easily.
and every time i hear them,
i often ignore the sound.
i think to myself
if all of you truly loved me,
then where the hell are you now?

(late every midnight)

memories for me
have always been like ghosts.
i'm mostly haunted by the things
you left behind,
restless under the moon.
broken promises are
scattered across the floors of my mind.
there are cracks and scars
on the surface of my heart.
yes, memories for me are like ghosts.
though others may not be able to see them,
i do. it's the memories of you,
of us, that keep me up at night.

(love lessons learned)

you taught me things
like how to survive
a broken heart,
how to smile
to keep from crying,
how to hide the pain
with laughter.
you taught me things
that only someone
like you could teach.
you taught me to want more,
so on the day that you return
throwing "I miss you"
and "I'm sorry" my way,
i'll put to use the lessons you gave me.
i won't take you back.

(new beginnings)

one day you just wake up
not just physically but emotionally.
you realize that those who hurt you
were never worth your tears
and those who fought with you
didn't deserve of an emotional
response.
it's sad but beautiful all at once.
emotional enlightenment.

(non-optional)

choose her.
stop treating her like an option.
stop neglecting the one who is
always there when others aren't.
put nothing above her.
choose her because
she's always choosing you.

(our end)

i just wanted it to be you—the one with whom i'd spend
the rest of my life,
the one next to whom i'd fall asleep and rise
each morning like the sun.
our love was far from perfect.
at times, you were my piece of heaven.
and it hurt like hell
when we both lost it all.

(Scars of Survival)

you let people in.
they destroy you, but you survive.
there are cracks in your heart
that only you can feel,
scars in places no one will ever see,
pain of which you may never even speak,
but you survived.

(she is you, she is strength)

she couldn't sleep.
she was too busy
telling her secrets
to midnight,
alone with just the moon
and anyone else.
too tired emotionally
to sleep.
but even in this brokenness,
she remained strong.
she's reading this now.
she is you, you are strength.
you're going to be fine.

(there's life in death)

i dug that grave myself.
it wasn't easy.
i took everything we used to be,
threw it in a box, nailed it shut,
and placed it in a pit
some place suitable for the failures
of our union.
so when you look for me,
find me there.
you'll discover all the things
you took for granted,
and you'll try to reenter my life
but find yourself at the exit.
my heart is filled to capacity with someone else.
no room for you,
just room for peace.
i found life in the death of us.

(we, my generation)

we don't want to be alone, yet we isolate ourselves.
we want people to fight for us, yet we easily walk away.
we want happiness, yet our minds dwell on things that
destroy peace.
we want to fall in love, yet we push away anyone who
attempts to provide it.
we...

(wishing well)

i hope you find someone capable of destroying you
but who would rather help build you up and inspire you
to grow.
i hope the person capable of becoming your weakness
chooses to be your strength when you need it.
i hope you find a love strong enough to hold your
heavy heart—
a love that sees the scars on your soul yet still thinks
you're beautiful.

SAMANTHA KING

Clarity

Maybe I'm not as okay as I want to believe.
Maybe those broken pieces I keep denying
are attracting the wrong souls—
souls who linger way too long, trying to take away
whatever light I have left. And I let them.
Maybe it's time to fess up that it's not them, it's me.

Devotion

May your heart never break.
But if it should, I'll be here to pick up the pieces.
May your soul never grow weary.
But if it should, may the light of my soul rejuvenate
yours.
May your legs never give out from under you.
But if they should, I will carry you wherever you need to
go.
May your hand never feel lonely.
But if it should, my friend, know that my hand is always
yours to hold.

Don't Quit

You don't stop walking
just because you fall.
You don't stop believing the sun will come
just because it won't stop raining.
You don't stop loving
just because your heart has been broken.
You don't stop dreaming
just because you fear you might fail.
So you shouldn't stop living
just because it isn't going as you planned.

Epiphany

I wanted to believe I was capable of making him
change.
That was my ignorance. It was only I who needed to be
different.

Fool Me Twice

I took a risk by reinvesting myself.
I took an even bigger one when I began to care.
But I tightened the knot of the noose around my neck
when I began to love you again.
You kicked the chair out from under me
so I didn't even have to jump.

For Brittany

Let my eyes be the guide to the labyrinth that is your soul.
Hold fast to my hand as I guide you past the screams of your insecurities—
the dead ends that are your fears.
I'll see this through and stay with you to the end
till we reach the illumination of all the beauty to which you've been blind.
When you look in the mirror, all you see is a pocket change
version of yourself
rather than the priceless gem I know you to be.
Negative thoughts run rampant
while peace tries to find you.
Discouraged by the constant bantering of false friends, you
begin to doubt whether you really are a good person.
"Good" will do no justice in defining you
and neither will "amazing"
for the depths of who you are couldn't be limited to the boundaries of a single word
no matter the language.
You and I so alike and yet so different—
similar struggles, different solutions.
The methods we've used before haven't worked.
It's time to take the risk in believing,
not just hoping.
The hardest part is trusting yourself enough to start.
I'm here. We're here.
No more looking back, dwelling on time that we can't fix.
The future is before us.
Let's not make it wait.

Goodbye

"I'm sorry" is no longer a healing balm.
"It won't happen again" is just another lie.
I see the remorse on your face.
It's just that I can no longer sympathize.
You've drained me of whatever ability I had left
to dig a little deeper and
believe this was worth saving.
I won't be staying tonight.
I won't be coming back tomorrow.
You can keep your watered-down promises of forever.

Intimacy

I rather you fall in love with my naked soul than my
naked body.
I am more than breasts and ass.
I am a sensation.
I am to be felt without being touched.
I am to be understood without being seen.

Obsession

Numb,
betrayed,
my mind is cloudy,
my heart is crowded,
the hum of the fan in the background is my new lifeline
to sanity.
I can't shake the emotions. The feelings,
they're grappling for my solace,
ripping at the threadbare remnants of my quiet
happiness.
How still, how simple, how beautiful it all was.
I can't keep doing this.
I don't know how to sustain.
Remaining in the fear of losing you, I'm losing me with
every passing second,
I'm waiting for them to come a-knocking.
A padded four-wall prison awaits me,
'cause between you and I,
I'm pretty sure I've gone crazy.
I wanted to embed myself in your life.
I tried. I tried too hard,
letting the beauty of who I am subside
to become what I thought you wanted me to be.
I failed at that and learned that
I'd rather crash and burn being me.

Reuben

He exists.
I think I just met him.
His soul was radiating against the backdrop of his
beautiful brown eyes.
I think he caught me staring.
It took all the restraint I had not to reach out and touch
the chocolate delicacy he calls skin.
He may be a saint, but the look of him entices sin.
I'm not blaming him; my imagination tends to get away
from me
'cause I've already thought about him undressed,
my head cradled in his hand as the sound of his heart
lulls me to sleep.
The reality of him—
his mind, the breath he's taking now,
the words he speaks, his melodious laugh,
that smile. His essence
is so much more enchanting than anything that I could
have ever conjured
in the sweetest of my dreams.
He has given me peace
I am fortunate to be in this moment and
blessed to have made his acquaintance.
I have given him nothing—
no secrets, no promises—and my heart remains mine
while he has given me everything.
Don't wake me up.
Whatever you do, don't wake me up.

Sweet Dreams

I prayed for strength when I should have asked for
wisdom.
I sought refuge between my sheets.
When slumber approaches, I escape into a place
where I have a clean slate and no inhibitions to hold
me back.
No judgement to be sought for my bad behavior
resides there,
just the quiet reassurance that, once the scene is
played out, it's really over.
No harm is caused, no battles are lost.
I'm not even awake to appreciate the time when I
actually live in the moment, the truest time.
Despite instability, I've always lived safe and
accomplished what I was told would make me feel
great. But now I'm empty,
never bold enough to believe in myself.
So I let other people lead me. Seems they sent me off
a cliff.
Now I've hit bottom, and funny thing about that
is I'm alone, not scared or battered, just tired and
waiting.
For what? I really don't know.
I just know I'm not quite ready to stand yet.
When we're young, we're taught how to walk, we're
taught what's right and wrong.
We're not taught how to live, we're taught what is
expected.

Untitled

I died a thousand deaths
trying to get you to love me once.
You never did.
There's a part of me that didn't survive "us".

Breaking Point

I screamed. You didn't hear me.
I walked away. You didn't chase.
I've found that our value lies not in what's spoken
between us
but in all the things your actions say.
I've cried more than I've smiled.
I've lost more than I've gained.
I'm tired of sacrificing, but no big fuss
'cause you won't even notice what's happened
until its already too late.

Me & You

So radiant, we're like stars—
souls so bright we can barely be contained,
so use to our own space that we don't know how to
share.
Let me be a part of your constellation.
Connect me to you.

The Endless Struggle

I write what I can't say.
I weep for these lost emotions—
these voiceless, unclaimed soldiers that go to battle
everyday
only to lose their lives, spilling out on to my cheeks.
So many casualties have been laid to rest upon my
pillow case.
What should bring my head solace is now a graveyard
for
abandoned feelings.

I sit up and work over and over in my mind.
Is there any logic to it all?
For that to truly exist, emotion would need to cease.
I struggle with the war that's continuing inside me as
we speak,
defined by impulsions, confined.

Underwater Mountains Publishing.
Elias Joseph Mennealy & Ryan Christopher Lutfalah.
A Private Company.

45759693R00027

Made in the USA
Charleston, SC
26 August 2015